BUTTERFINGERS

For Susan Dickinson

This edition published 1997 by
Diamond Books
77-85 Fulham Palace Road
Hammersmith, London W6 8JB

First published in Great Britain 1991 by William Collins Sons & Co Ltd
First published in Picture Lions 1993

ISBN 0 26166 955 9

Printed by International Printing House, Egypt

BUTTERFINGERS

Dennis Reader

Benjamin Butters was known to everybody as Butterfingers.
He was always dropping things.

"It's as if his fingers were covered in butter,"
said Mrs Butters.
"Or margarine," said Mr Butters.

Benjamin dropped his toast butter-side down,
usually on the dog...

and the pet goldfish on the cat.

All of this was a great worry to Mrs Butters, who was soon expecting another baby.

Mr Butters said he'd have his work cut out worrying about the new baby, so Benjamin should stay with his grandparents for a while.

Grandad and Grandma Butters lived on a small farm
that smelled of pigs and cows and chickens because
that's what they kept and it was super.

Grandad Butters once let Benjamin collect the eggs.
Afterwards Grandad Butters said once was enough.

Grandma Butters said Benjamin could feed Pauline the pig.
"After all," she said, "you can't slop slops!"

But Benjamin could...

And after Druscilla the cow gave her best bucket
of milk in a lifetime...

Benjamin somehow tipped it all over the duck.

So, if you were able to ask...

the Butters' dog...

the Butters' cat...

any chicken...

the Butters' goldfish...

the duck...

Pauline the pig...

...or Druscilla the cow if Benjamin was a bit of a butterfingers they would be inclined to agree.

One day Grandma Butters took a phone call that
made her very happy.
"You've got a new baby sister," she told Benjamin.
"You can soon go home."

Benjamin wasn't sure if the news of her granddaughter
had made Grandma happy or if it was because he
was going home.

Anyway he tried not to drop too many things before he left.

When Benjamin and Grandad and Grandma arrived there were uncles and aunts Benjamin couldn't remember ever having seen before...

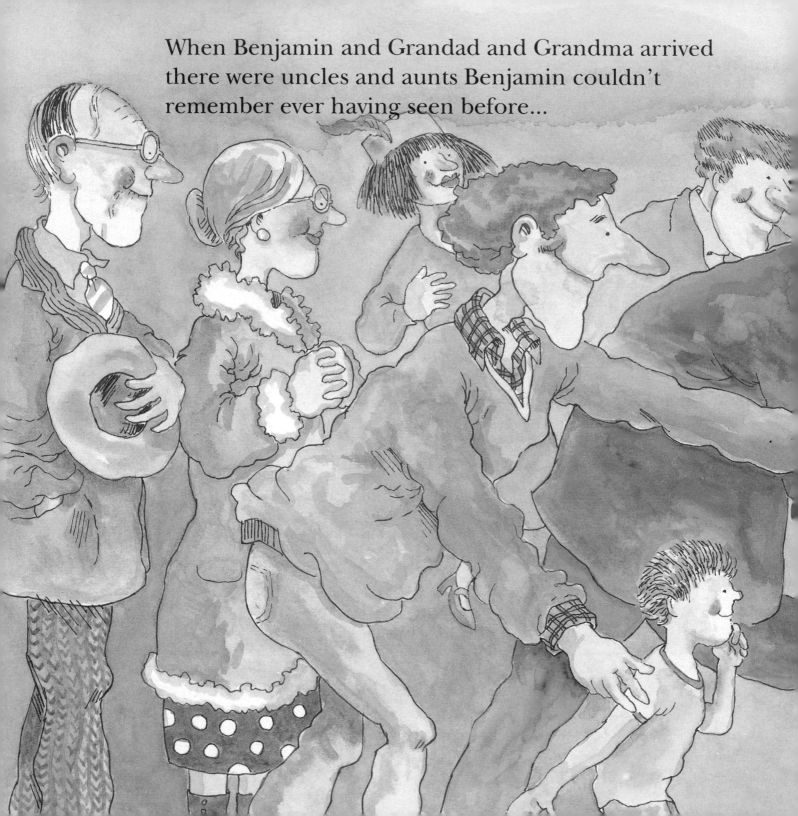

...and they were all making strange noises and poking their fingers at the baby, who wiggled her toes and seemed to quite enjoy it.

"Come and meet your new baby sister," said Benjamin's mum.

She was almost as pink as the baby and looked very happy.

Benjamin looked closely at the baby.   She had eyes like
screwed-up blackcurrants.
"Can I hold her?" he asked his mum.

Benjamin's dad went rigid in a kind of way...the uncles and aunts and grandparents seemed to stop breathing as Benjamin's mum said, "Of course you can... but be careful..."

Benjamin tucked his arms under the baby and held her
to him. She was woolly warm. Her fingers gripped
tight around his. And then she smiled at him.

It was a wonderful smile.

Baby Butters knew she was safe.
Benjamin wasn't going to drop her.

She was his sister.

THE WILD GARDEN BOOK

Contents

Written by Ron Wilson
Illustrated by Simone Robertson and Ann Alexander

Collins Educational
An imprint of HarperCollinsPublishers

Introduction

A wildlife garden is any area, large or small, where we can use plants to attract insects, birds and mammals. By doing this and thinking carefully about what is around us, we can become more aware of our environment and how to improve it.

There are various ways to attract more wildlife. The plans and illustrations in this book will help you choose the best way to make the most of existing areas by improving plant life and wildlife activity.

First you need to plan your garden. Draw a plan of the area you wish to develop, showing any features already there. If the area is large, you might be able to establish more than one **habitat** such as 'A Pond Garden' (see pages 20-25) and 'A Bird Garden' (see pages 26-31). In a small garden or area, you may decide to have 'An 'Instant' Garden' (see pages 32-34).

Planning a school wildlife garden can involve many people: pupils, teachers and parents. You might also seek the advice of voluntary groups, like the Wildlife Trust or the British Trust for Conservation Volunteers.

Making a wildlife garden is both fun and rewarding. Now you are ready to plan a wildlife garden of your own, so enjoy yourself!

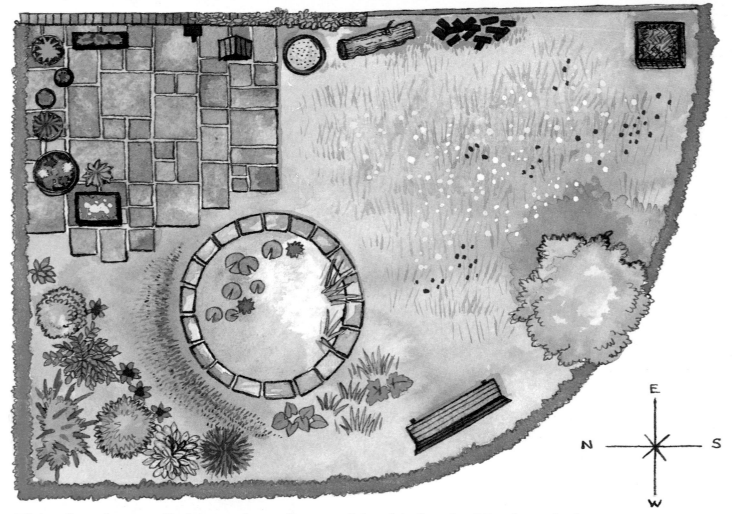

This plan shows all the gardens discussed in this book. Use it to help you choose which garden you wish to plan, and which is most suitable for your area.

3

A Butterfly, Moth and Bee Garden

If you choose the right kinds of plants, you can attract many insects to your area, whatever its size.

The best flowers for attracting insects are those which produce a lot of **nectar**. A well-planned butterfly, moth and bee garden has flowers from spring through to autumn to provide food.

The early flowers provide nectar when the insects wake up from **hibernation,** and in autumn, butterflies take their supplies of nectar before they hibernate. You may see small peacock, tortoise-shell, cabbage white, red admiral and brimstone butterflies at this time of year. If you have limited space, planting a buddleia – the 'butterfly bush' – may be the easiest way to attract all these insects.

Unlike butterflies which feed during the day, moths feed at night. To attract insects such as the hawkmoth, plant night-scented plants.

You can choose to plant a butterfly, moth and bee garden in a border, in window boxes and in tubs on balconies, window ledges or paved areas.

4

TO PLANT A BUTTERFLY, MOTH AND BEE GARDEN:

Site and size: south or southwest-facing. Make sure all flowers for butterflies are planted in a sunny spot, out of the wind.

Suggested plants: perennials are the best value as they will grow again, year after year. **Annuals** will grow for only one year.

YOU WILL NEED:

fork, spade, trowel, **compost** or fertilizer, **bark mulch** or wood chippings

---

Tall plants: angelica, fennel, foxglove (perennial), hollyhock, sunflower and teasel (perennial).

Medium height plants: bluebell (perennial), corn cockle, cornflower, cranesbill (perennial), honesty, lavender, michaelmas daisy, nasturtium, ox-eye daisy, phlox, poppy, red campion, scabious, toadflax, valerian and wallflower.

Low plants: alyssum, aubretia, bird's foot trefoil, celandine, clover, cowslip, harebell (perennial), herb robert, primrose and winter aconite.

Creeping plants: bugle, scarlet pimpernel, selfheal, thyme and wild strawberry.

Night-scented plants: evening primrose, everlasting pea, honeysuckle, night-scented catchfly, night-scented stock, petunia, soapwort and valerian.

HOW TO PLANT:

1 Prepare the soil by removing weeds and adding compost or fertilizer.

2 Plan the position of the plants. Put the tallest at the back and the lowest at the front to make sure the lower plants are not smothered.

3 Plant with a trowel, firming the soil with your fingers. Water well.

4 Place bark mulch or wood chippings round the plants to discourage weeds.

AFTERCARE:

Water the plants regularly, especially in dry weather, and remove any weeds. Let the flowers seed after flowering. Collect

some seeds for **germination** the following year (see Diary – August). Leave the remaining seeds for the birds.

Snails and slugs may nibble at the leaves, so to limit the damage they cause, put crushed eggshells round the base of the plants. Slugs and snails avoid moving over rough surfaces and will be deterred from reaching the plants.

In digesting plant matter, worms make the soil **fertile** and **aerate** it, and so these, too, should be left. Leave ladybirds to control the **larvae** of greenfly. Remember, never use chemical sprays on your patch as these could harm the wildlife. There are safe alternatives, and in most cases the animals in your garden will keep the pests at bay.

9

A Wild Flower Garden

Any area of rough grass can be made more attractive to insects and **invertebrates**, by turning it into a wild flower garden.

Before planning a wild flower area, you need to know what plants are there already. If the grass has been mown, try not to cut it for a year and observe what happens when it is left to grow naturally. Keep a list of all the plants, such as daisies, clover and dandelions, which appear. If it is a lawn or playing field it may not be as exciting as a piece of grassland in the country, but you might be surprised.

Look closely for grasshoppers and other invertebrates which may be present in long grass, and for cuckoo spit, made by the froghopper bug, which may be seen on longer plant stems in late spring and summer.

Scattering wild flower seeds on grass or the surface of hard ground won't improve your area, because the grass prevents seeds from germinating and the birds eat them. The best way is to plant out wild flowers, either grown yourself from seed or bought from a nursery.

You can also plant a wild flower garden of grasses and

flowers in pots and containers to brighten small areas (see An 'Instant' Garden, pages 32-34).

To plant a wild flower garden:

Site and size: almost any area of grassland is suitable but preferably it should be a minimum of 5m x 5m. Always make sure the plants are native species because they grow best in the conditions they have been used to. You must not take flowers from the roadside or parks without the owner's permission, and uprooting wild flowers is illegal.

You will need:

spade, trowel,
peat substitute, water

Suggested plants:
Light: common cat's ear, field poppy, hardheads, kidney vetch, lady's bedstraw, meadow buttercup, rough hawkbit, salad burnet, soapwort, wild marjoram, yarrow, yellow rattle.

Shade: archangel, bluebell, field scabious, lesser celandine, primrose, sweet violet, wood anemone, wood sorrel.

Grasses: meadow foxtail, timothy.

How to plant:

1 Dig out squares of **turf**, 30cm x 30cm where you are going to put the plants.

2 Remove the top 10cm of soil, which may be too **fertile** for wild flower seeds, and replace with a peat substitute.

3 Dig a hole in the square with a trowel.

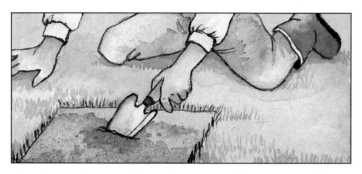

4 Carefully lift the plant from the pot to avoid damaging the roots. Follow any special instructions on the plant label.

5 Firm the soil with your fingers and then water well.

AFTERCARE:

Water the plants daily for at least the first two weeks unless the weather is very wet.

A Tree Garden

Trees provide **habitats** for many insects, **invertebrates**, birds and small mammals, both on and in the tree, and also in the leaf litter beneath.

14

Birds use trees as a perch, and insects might lay their eggs on leaves and bark in the spring.

The marble gall wasp may lay her eggs on oak trees. You can see where the eggs are by the round growths left where buds were.

Trees also attract hedgehogs. They eat the **grubs** of various insects which live in amongst the plants and leaf litter under the tree. Hedgehogs have well-developed senses of smell and hearing which help them to detect and eat pests, and this helps the gardener.

To encourage hedgehogs, provide them with additional food in late summer and early autumn. Do not feed them milk because this upsets their digestive system. Leave tinned cat or dog food on a saucer outside each evening and observe any visitors which may come for the food.

Other small mammals attracted to trees are not as easy to identify as they move very quickly and many are **nocturnal**. These animals may include house mice, black rats, bank voles, long-tailed field (or wood) mice, yellow-necked mice and pygmy or common shrews.

Some small mammals attracted to trees, like rats, are best kept out of the garden, and squirrels and mice can also be a nuisance.

The best time for planting trees is between November and March when they are **dormant**. Trees can be carefully moved at this time without doing them any harm. Try not to plant them when the weather is too cold or windy, or if the ground is **waterlogged** or frozen.

Some trees are slow-growing, and a large oak could measure up to 30m in height, and have a **canopy** of great spread. Smaller, faster-growing trees, such as alder or silver birch, may be a sensible alternative if space is limited.

Planting a tree could be linked to National Tree Week, which takes place every November. It is an ideal way to mark a school event or anniversary.

16

To plant a tree:

Site and size: not too close to a pond, buildings, walls or areas of **asphalt** as root spread can cause damage. For tall trees such as oak, choose a large, open space with an area of 15m radius round the tree.

Suggested plants: native species are the best for wildlife, e.g., alder, beech, rowan, silver birch, oak (buy 60-90cm **whips**).

HOW TO PLANT:

Pot grown trees should be kept in containers until you are ready to plant them. Bare-rooted trees should be kept in **polythene** bags, making sure the roots are kept moist.

1 Dig a hole big enough for the roots. Put the soil to one side, for use later. Loosen the soil in the bottom of the hole.

2 Trees taller than 1.5m will need staking. Use a sharpened stake, about 2.5cm square and the same height as the tree. Using a mallet, drive it into the ground to one side of the hole.

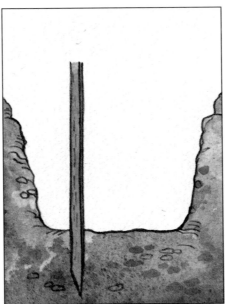

3 With help, put the tree into the hole and spread out the roots. Make sure the soil mark on the tree trunk is level with the top of the ground.

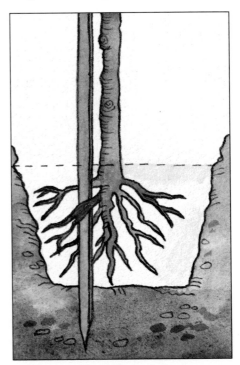

4 Mix the fertilizer with the **topsoil**. Put small amounts into the hole, gently shaking the tree as you do so, to fill the spaces between the roots. After filling the hole a quarter full, gently trample the soil down with your heel. Add more soil, firming each spadeful, until the hole is full.

5 Attach the tree to the stake with a tree tie. Put the tree guard round the tree to encourage faster growth and protect the tree from animals. Put down approximately 5cm of bark mulch or wood chippings for a radius of 30-40cm away from the trunk, then water and allow to settle in.

AFTERCARE:

Your tree will grow well, especially during the first two years of life. Water once a week from spring to autumn in the first year. Make sure the soil around the tree stays firm and doesn't crack or become loose around the trunk, and check the stakes and tie. After a minimum of two years, remove the stake – the tree should be strong enough not to need further support.

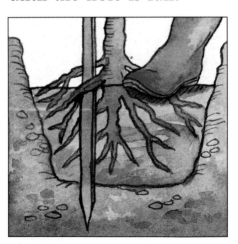

A Pond Garden

Building a pond, whatever its size, will attract different insects and **invertebrates** from those attracted to a 'dry' garden.

Areas of water provide a place for frogs, toads or newts to **spawn**. Many flying **aquatic** creatures, including great diving beetles, whirligig beetles and water boatmen, will live by the pond, and dragonflies, caddisflies and mayflies lay eggs in it.

You can provide different plants to attract different creatures. **Submerged** plants produce oxygen in the water

which is important for fish, snails and other waterlife. **Free-floating** plants add shelter and shade for various creatures, whilst **emergent** plants growing out of the water also provide shelter. **Edging** plants can be planted directly into the soil round the edge of the pond, both hiding the pond liner and providing cover for many insects and **amphibians**.

There are various ways of making a pond garden and you do not, necessarily, need a large area. If space is limited, old baths or sinks with blocked up plugholes make suitable ponds. In larger areas, the pond should be on a sloping site to make it suitable for different aquatic creatures and, if possible, have a marshy area made from very damp soil along one side.

Ponds need topping up, especially in hot weather, so a source of water nearby is also important.

With fewer natural ponds in the countryside, garden ponds are becoming more important for wildlife. This is an ideal project for building at school, although adult help will be needed.

To make a pond:

Site and size: sunny and, if possible, protected from the north wind. Don't put the pond under a tree, as when leaves rot they may **pollute** the water, killing wildlife. Ponds other than bath or sink ponds should be a minimum of 1m long, 75cm wide and 60cm deep.

Suggested plants:
Submerged: bladderwort, hornwort,
water milfoil and water starwort.

Free-floating plants: frogbit and
water crowfoot.

Emergent plants: arrowhead, flowering
rush, watercress, water plantain, water
violet and yellow flag iris.

Edging plants: hemp agrimony, marsh
marigold or kingcup, marsh woundwort,
mints, water forget-me-not and
water speedwell.

HOW TO BUILD A POND:

1 Plan the pool shape on graph paper,
and work out the area of liner you need –
the width of the liner equals pond width
plus twice the maximum depth; the
length of the liner equals pond length
plus twice the maximum depth. Decide
where you are going to put the soil dug
from the hole. It could be used to make a
bank to shelter the pond.

2 Mark out the shape of the pond on the ground using the stakes and string, then take off the **turf**. (This could be used round the edge later.) The shapes made by the edge should be smooth, otherwise fitting the liner will be a problem.

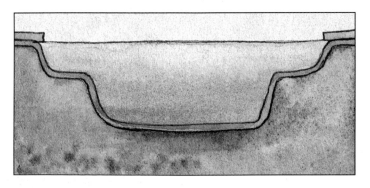

3 Dig the hole, starting in the middle and sloping the sides. The hole should be about 15cm deeper than the final depth of the pond to allow for sand, carpet, etc., with a ledge 10cm below the top edge for emergent plants.

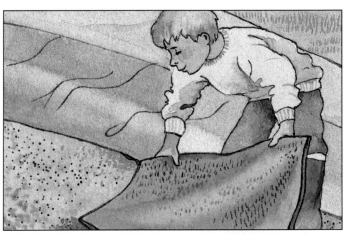

4 Take out any sharp stones. Smooth the sides, and spread a layer of fine sand 5-6cm deep in the bottom. Then lay old carpet or newspaper on top of this and over the sides.

6 Put the liner in position. Make sure that it covers the bottom and sides. Use the concrete slabs to hold the liner in place on the edge (ask an adult for help).

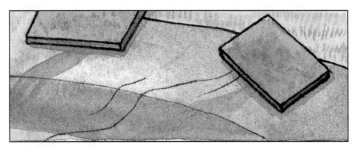

7 Put about 10cm of **topsoil** on the liner. Take out any sharp stones.

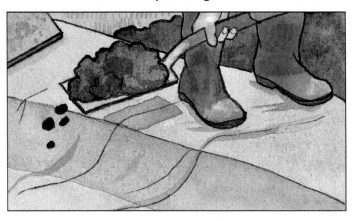

8 Rest the hose on an old piece of matting in the bottom of the pond. This stops the soil from being disturbed as the pond fills. Slowly fill with water, leaving 2.5cm space at the top. The weight of the water will mould the liner to the shape of the hole.

9 Trim the liner, leaving 15–20cm around the edge.

10 Place concrete slabs round the edge, to hold it down permanently (ask an adult for help). These should hang over the edge about 5cm, to give a neater effect and allow a hiding place for snails, etc. You could also use some of the turf to hide the liner.

PLANTING:

The best time to plant is May and June. Choose a mixture of submerged, free-floating, emergent and edging plants. Submerged plants need to be in plastic containers with mesh sides. A layer of **shingle** on top of the soil will prevent it from being washed out.

AFTERCARE:

There is no need to feed the creatures in the pond. As it becomes established, the **organisms** will feed on each other.

In hot weather, replace water lost by evaporation.

Algae should be removed as it appears, otherwise it will prevent light from penetrating the water.

In the autumn, check plant growth so that the pond does not become overcrowded. Also take out excess weed.

Tree leaves will rot away, but very slowly, so don't allow too many to get into the pond.

If ice forms, place a container on the surface and fill with boiling water. Repeat this until it melts a hole in the ice, allowing gases, which are harmful to fish, to escape. Don't break the ice as it could injure fish.

A Bird Garden

You can make a garden that will attract different kinds of birds and there are various ways to do this.

To place a free-standing bird-feeding table:

1 Dig a hole about 30cm deep to take the post.
2 If necessary, attach the top of the free-standing table and the roof to the post after fixing the post in the ground.

To place a hanging bird-feeding table:

1 Screw the bracket to the wall at least 1.5m above the ground.
2 Hang the chain from the bracket.
3 Hang the bird-feeding table from the chain.

TO PLACE A DUST AND WATER BATH:

YOU WILL NEED:

spade, two dustbin lids
or large bowls, fine dry soil, water

1 To make either bath, dig a hole in the ground large enough to take the dustbin lid or bowl.

2 Put a dustbin lid or bowl in the hole.

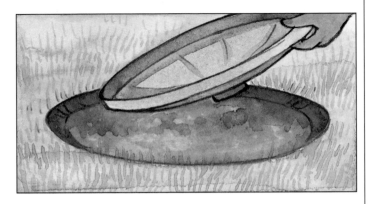

3 Fill one with dust for a dust bath, and the other with water for a water bath.

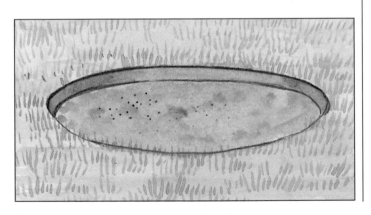

AFTERCARE:

Always check the bird-feeding table for food which has been left (especially any scraps of meat), and clean it occasionally. This prevents rats and mice causing a problem, and it also ensures the birds won't catch diseases.

Fill the water bath with water regularly when the level drops and break any ice that forms during the winter as the water will also be used for drinking.

Keep the dust bath topped up with dry soil.

An 'Instant' Garden

THE CONTAINER GARDEN

You don't need a garden to attract wildlife; any small area such as a window sill can be turned into a suitable **habitat**.

Use tubs, plastic or earthenware containers, old chimney pots, or stone sinks planted with flowers to attract insects to a paved area. If you are planting wild flowers elsewhere, it is a good idea to put the same flowers in the containers to keep the insects interested in the wildlife area for longer. If you want to attract butterflies and bees, then use some of the plants suggested on pages 5-7.

Most plants, except for the tree or pond plants, are suitable for planting in containers, but when buying plants, look at the labels for flowering times so that you have a succession of **blooms**.

PLANTING A CONTAINER:

Site and size: choose plants according to whether they will be in sun or shade and the size of the container.

YOU WILL NEED:

containers with drainage holes in the bottom, trowel, stones or broken pottery, multi-purpose soil, water

---

Suggested plants: any from 'A Butterfly, Moth and Bee Garden' (see pages 4-9) or 'A Wild Flower Garden' (see pages 10-13).

HOW TO PLANT:

1 Put a few stones or pieces of broken pottery in the bottom of the container for drainage.

2 Half fill the container with soil.

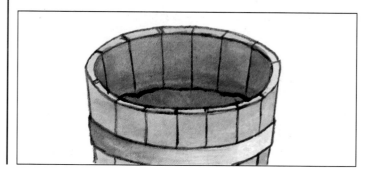

3 Gently remove plants from their pots, taking note of any special instructions.

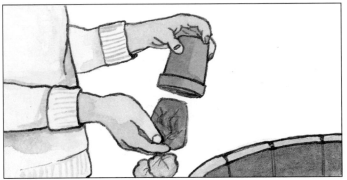

4 Place plants in the container, allowing space between each one for growth.

5 Add more soil to fill the container to 1cm below the rim, and water thoroughly.

AFTERCARE:

Containers dry out much faster than soil in the ground, so make sure they stay moist, especially during dry weather. You might need to water them every day in the summer. Remove any weeds and **dead head** flowers to prolong flowering.

The 'Unplanned' Garden

Wildlife will be attracted to areas you might not think of as a garden and you can encourage these creatures further.

DEADWOOD PILES

Damp, rotting wood provides a good multi-storey **habitat** for wildlife. In a well-established pile, there may be as many as 1,000 different species of **invertebrates** in residence. In turn, these provide food for birds and small mammals like shrews.

If the wood dries out, **larvae** living there might die, so the pile must remain damp. The logs should not be too close to living trees and plants because the fungi and **bacteria** causing the rotting could spread to them. If there is bark on the log, leave this to provide a cool hiding place for some invertebrates.

BRICKS AND STONES

Piles of bricks, with spaces left between them, provide hiding places and homes for invertebrates such as snails, slugs, earwigs and woodlice.

CORRUGATED IRON

This isn't as readily available as it was in the past, but if you can find a piece, put it down in a rough area to provide a suitable habitat for various creatures. Apart from many invertebrates, voles and mice might also find a home. If you lift it up carefully, you can often see small mammal tunnels through the grass.

SACKING AND MATTING

Placed in various out-of-the-way, shady and sheltered places, invertebrates find shelter here.

FLOWER POTS

Upturned earthenware flowerpots, and those half-buried in the soil, provide homes for many invertebrates.

Using a Wall

You can attract wildlife to a new wall by using it to support climbing plants. Once the plants grow they will provide **habitats** for **invertebrates**, spiders, birds, and perhaps small mammals.

Climbers are also suitable for small birds such as thrushes and hedge sparrows to nest in, and there are likely to be many other winter hibernators, including small tortoiseshell butterflies. Brimstone butterflies may also spend the winter there. They look just like dead ivy leaves, and once settled in the autumn, they are very well **camouflaged**.

Plants such as wall rue, maidenhair spleenwort, ferns and lichen often grow between cracks in older walls and large numbers of invertebrates will seek shelter there. Solitary bees may find a place and spiders will certainly be attracted to these **crevices**. The damper places offer shelter for snails and for many other creatures, including woodlice. Rotting leaves and wood at the bottom of the wall also provides them with food.

From about November, ivy flowers will provide **nectar** for many insects, including late butterflies still on the wing. Once the flowers of ivy have been pollinated, the berries start to develop which then provide a valuable supply of food for some winter birds.

Using a Hedge

A hedge will provide food and shelter for a variety of small mammals, **invertebrates** and insects. If the hedge is new, you can encourage wildlife to visit by planting wild flowers.

One of the earliest wild flowers to come into **bloom** is the garlic mustard, also called jack-by-the-hedge. The flowers provide **nectar** for some of the first butterflies and bees to come out of **hibernation**. It is also useful as a food plant for the orange-tip butterfly.

If you plant a hawthorn hedge, it will produce flowers and nectar for insects in the spring, and berries for birds in the autumn. They may visit the hedge very soon after planting and mature hedges will provide nesting places for birds such as song thrushes, blackbirds, hedge sparrows and chaffinches.

Small mammals, like mice, shrews, voles and rabbits, find shelter in the bottom of the hedge and hedgehogs might also hibernate there. Once the leaves appear on the hawthorn, some moths lay their eggs. At least one hundred different species of moth caterpillars feed on hawthorn shoots and leaves in spring.

Compost

Compost is a rich material which you can recycle from **biodegradable** household and garden waste, and reuse in the garden as fertilizer.

A compost heap provides shelter for a large number of **invertebrates**, including woodlice, snails, slugs, millipedes, centipedes, spiders, beetles, etc. and occasionally a grass snake or slowworm might lay eggs. Because some animals live there, other animals will come to feed on them.

To make a compost heap, start with a layer of vegetable matter and grass clippings, then cover this with a layer of soil. Repeat these layers alternately over a period of time. When the heap is 1–1.5m high, cover it with a piece of old carpet or sacking.

It is best to place the compost heap in a shady corner of the garden, and to use materials which **decompose** quite quickly, like vegetable matter, rotten fruit, old newspapers etc. Some garden material, like twigs and branches, isn't suitable for the compost heap as it takes a long time to **decay**.

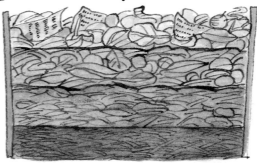

The compost heap will look after itself. The material in the compost heap will decay and much of this is brought about by small plants and animals eating the matter, digesting it and excreting it. Then the compost can be used on your garden when putting in new plants.

DIARY

JANUARY
Always make sure that there is food out for birds. Fieldfares and redwings (winter visiting thrushes) will come into the garden when it is very cold and food is scarce. Put out apples for them to peck at. Always leave water out, using a small 'stove' with a night light underneath to stop the water from freezing. Keep a diary of the birds which come to your wildlife garden.

FEBRUARY
In a mild winter the first butterflies might be out. Make a note of the date. They will be seeking **nectar** from any early flowers. Early nesting birds will be searching for places to build. If you see robins, watch for their **territorial** displays. Watch blackbirds chasing each other from the garden.

MARCH
More butterflies will come out. The first birds nest this month. Make a note of any new visitors and whether they have begun nesting. Nests are vulnerable at this time of the year when there are no leaves on the trees - apart from the evergreens.

If growing wild flowers, etc. from seeds, check when they need to be planted.

APRIL
Keep a note of which spring flowers are the most popular with butterflies and insects. Depending on the weather, birds may already be using any nestboxes.

MAY
Get up early and go into the garden to listen to the **dawn chorus**. Look around your pond for mayflies which emerge this month.

JUNE
Watch bumblebees visiting flowers. Note how they sit on flowers like white deadnettles and how they get into other flowers. Check nestboxes, but be careful not to disturb the occupants; it is an offence to disturb nesting birds.

JULY
Keep the pond topped up especially in hot weather. Ensure birds have food, dust and water. Look out for wasps and hoverflies. A good month to look for moths.

AUGUST
Collect wild flower seeds from the dead flowerheads. Never pull up plants from the countryside. Put seed heads in paper bags and hang up to dry.

SEPTEMBER
Change the bird food diet. Most birds will have finished breeding by now.

Leave any seedheads for birds to peck at. Put out tinned dog food for hedgehogs. Watch flowers for butterflies.

OCTOBER
Check and clean out nestboxes. You may find other residents than birds, like bumblebees or even field mice. Collect **haws** from hawthorn this month or next.

NOVEMBER
Ensure you continue to provide food, water and dust for birds. Clear up leaves and dead plants and put them on the **compost** heap.

DECEMBER
Keep ponds and bird baths free of frost. Bring in any scraps of food which haven't been eaten by birds. Make puddings for the birds from leftovers such as bread and fat from the kitchen.

FURTHER READING

Birdfeeder Handbook (*Dorling Kindersley*): Robert Burton.

Clue Books (*Oxford University Press*): Insects; Tracks and Signs; Birds; Flowers; Trees; Freshwater Animals; Flowerless Plants.

Collins Gem Guides: Butterflies and Moths; Birds; Wild Animals; Wild Flowers.

Discovering Nature in Your Town (*Earthkind*): Ron Wilson.

The Easy Way to Bird Recognition (*Kingfisher*): John Kilbracken.

The Easy Way to Wild Flower Recognition (*Kingfisher*): John Kilbracken.

Eyewitness Guides (*Dorling Kindersley*): Bird; Tree; Pond and River; Butterfly and Moth; Woodland; Plant and Flower; Mammal.

Junior Nature Guides (*Dragons World*): Trees; Wild Flowers; Insects; Mammals.

Kingfisher Guides (*Kingfisher*): Birds; Trees; Wild Flowers; Butterflies.

Land and Water Invertebrates – Identification in the School Grounds (*Southgate*): Lynette Merrick.

The Nature Trail Books (*Usborne*): Birdwatching; Garden Wildlife; Insect Watching; Ponds and Streams; Trees and Leaves; Wild Animals.

Practical Conservation Pack for Teachers, BTCV, 36 St Mary's Street, Wallingford, Oxon, OX10 0UE.

Spotters Guides (*Usborne*): Animal Tracks and Signs; Town and City Wildlife; Birds; Butterflies; Garden Flowers; Insects; Trees; The Weather.

Starting Ecology (*Wayland*): Pond and Stream; Wasteland.

Whittet Natural History Books: Garden Creepy Crawlies; Hedgehogs; Bats; Frogs and Toads; Spiders; Robins; Pond Life; Mice and Voles; Urban Foxes; Squirrels. Details from Whittet Books, 1 Ainley Road, London W14 0BY.

USEFUL ADDRESSES

*Animal Rescue Organisations
British Hedgehog Preservation Society,
Knowbury House, Knowbury, Ludlow,
Shropshire, SY8 3JT.
Earthlings, Humane Education Centre, Avenue
Lodge, Bounds Green Road, London N22 4EU.
English Nature, Northminster House,
Peterborough, PE1 1UA. Tel: 01733 340345.
*Wildlife Trust (County Naturalists Trust,
Trusts for Nature Conservation).

EQUIPMENT AND SUPPLIES

Wildlife Watch, Royal Society for Nature
Conservation, The Green, Witham Park,
Waterside South, Lincoln, LN5 7JR.
Tel: 01522 544400.
Young Ornithologists Club (YOC), Royal
Society for the Protection of Birds, The Lodge,
Sandy, Beds, SG19 2DL. Tel: 01767 680551.

CJ Wildbird Foods Ltd, The Rea, Upton
Magna, Shrewsbury, SY4 4UB.
John Chambers (seeds), 15 Westleigh Road,
Barton Seagrave, Kettering, Northants,
NN15 5AJ.
Landlife Wild Flowers Ltd, The Old Police
Station, Lark Lane, Liverpool, L17 8UU.
Naturescape, Little Orchard, Whaton in Vale,
Notts, NG13 9EP.
Ronaash Root Trainers, Kersquarter, Kelso,
Roxburghshire, TD5 8HH.
RSPB Sales, The Lodge, Sandy, Beds,
SG19 2DL.
School Garden Company, PO Box 49,
Spalding, Lincs, PE11 1NZ.
Suffolk Herbs, Monks Farm, Coggenshall
Road, Kelvendon, Essex, CO5 9PG.

* See local telephone directory or library
for addresses and telephone numbers.

INDEX

GLOSSARY

aerate to encourage the presence of air

algae plants which contain chlorophyll but do not have stems, e.g., seaweed

amphibian creatures which live on land but breed in water, e.g., frogs, toads

annual a plant which completes its life cycle once a year

aquatic creatures or plants which live or grow in water

asphalt paving material made from crushed stone and tar

bacteria single-cell creatures

bark mulch half-rotten vegetable matter

biodegradable can be decomposed by bacteria

bloom the flowers on a plant

butyl very strong artificial material

camouflage the colouring of a creature which enables it to hide in a background

canopy highest level of tree branches

compost mixture of organic materials used as fertilizer

crevice small crack in rocks or between bricks

dawn chorus the sound of birds singing as dawn breaks

dead head to remove dead flowers from the plant

decay to rot as a result of bacterial or fungal action

decompostion see decay

dormant alive, but not growing

edging plants to be placed along an edge to finish it

emergent plants with roots in the water and stem and leaves above the water

fertile having nutrients to support plant growth

free-floating plants with roots not attached to anything

germination to sprout or grow from seed